Your Dog and Your Baby
— A Practical Guide —

by Silvia Hartmann-Kent

Illustrations by ZAK

D1297486

Third Edition
Revised

Howln Moon Press

Your Dog and Your Baby
— A Practical Guide —
Third Edition, Revised

by Silvia Hartmann-Kent
Illustrations by ZAK

First published by Dog House Publications, United Kingdom

Copyright 1999 by Silvia Hartmann-Kent
ISBN 1-888994-13-4

Published by Howln Moon Press
203 State Road, PO Box 238, Eliot, ME 03903
207-439-3508
Printed and bound in the United States

Library of Congress Cataloging-in-Publication Data
Hartmann-Kent, Silvia.
     Your dog and your baby : a practical guide / by Silvia Hartmann-Kent :
        illustrations by ZAK. -- 3rd. ed., rev.
     p. cm.
     Includes bibliographical references.
     ISBN 1-888994-13-4 (pbk.)
     1. Dogs -- Training. 2. Dogs -- Social aspects. 3. Children and animals.
        1. Title.
SF431.H328 1999
636.7'0887 - - dc21
                                            99-30729
                                             CIP

Contents • • • • • • • • • • • • • • • • • •

Foreword

by John Fisher — Co-founder, A.P.B.C., C.O.A.P.E.

In this priceless guide, Silvia Hartmann-Kent combines her knowledge of dogs with her knowledge of being a mother.

Never before has there been such a need for the information contained in these pages. With the recent bad publicity given to dogs, more and more mothers are becoming concerned about the relationship between their dogs and their children. As Silvia rightly points out, there really is no need to worry, providing the right kind of preparation, introduction and stress free training procedures have been carried out.

The emphasis throughout is on prevention. The guide encourages parents to anticipate problems, and suggests ways of guarding against them. Where there is already a problem, her "Action Plans" will show parents how to overcome them.

None of the methods described involve any kind of physical confrontation with the dog — they are based upon the building of trust between the parent, the dog and the child or baby.

The major cause for concern is how to introduce a new baby into a household where there is already a resident dog.

Many perfectly well adjusted dogs have to go through the trauma of being rehomed and some are unfortunately put to sleep simply because the parents to be are unsure how the dog will react and are understandably not prepared to take any risks. This guide will allay their fears and give them a positive program to follow which will result in a successful introduction and the formation of a long lasting bond.

As a canine behaviorist, I know that the subjects covered in this guide really do relate to the questions mothers and mothers-to-be want to know about, because they are the very questions most frequently asked of me.

Now that Silvia has collated them, I personally will find it extremely useful in my day to day practice of dealing with the problem behavior of pet dogs, especially where young children are involved.

First Edition Dedication

Some of my fondest childhood memories relate to an old mongrel who belonged to my aunt. He was my playmate, my protector and my best friend. He also taught me about taking responsibility for a fellow creature.

My children have their own best friends now — Alex aged nine has a black German Shepherd female called Rio who sleeps by his bed at night; Stephen aged one has a White Miniature Poodle puppy called Sweep who can always cheer him up simply by walking into the room and staying close to him.

I cannot start to thank our dogs for all they have taught my children; be it patience, learning to see things from a different point of view, perseverance and self confidence, but most of all a realistic regard and esteem for animals a million miles away from the sickly sweet 'little angels in furry outfits' image today's children are subjected to every time they switch on the television.

In owning and caring for a dog we experience first hand what it is like to be responsible for a small part of creation. Owning a dog entails much more commitment, time and trouble than owning a hamster or a goldfish, but the relationship we develop with our dog is correspondingly deeper and far more satisfying.

Interacting with the family dog is in many cases today the closest we and our children can get to staying in touch with nature itself — true nature that is, not a shallow and sentimental Hollywood version thereof.

I firmly believe dogs are good for people, and I know dogs can be good for children. All it takes is a little foresight and some sympathetic guidance by the parent to create a worthwhile partnership that will become part of your own child's fondest memories in the years to come.

Introduction to the Second Edition

I would like to welcome you sincerely to this new and revised edition of *Your Dog and Your Baby*.

No other book I have written since has received so much response — I have boxes and boxes of letters from women and grandparents all over the world, thanking me.

This is nice, because I always knew there was a need for this book.

I knew this because I have spent hours on the telephone, trying to reassure pregnant and very distraught women that they don't have to put the dog down just because there's a baby on the way —it seems there's always someone ready and willing to dole out this particular piece of bad advice.

Sometimes it was mother-in-law, sometimes a neighbor, sometimes a midwife or a health visitor with a dog phobia, but in every case, it made the parents in question feel terrible because they loved their dogs and felt in their hearts of hearts that their children would love them, too.

I wrote to many publishers at the time, and they all said the same thing — it'll never sell, who needs it, no thank you. Well, the last two editions are sold out, and that's a good thing because it gave me the opportunity to bring this book up to date and in line with the latest thinking on companion dogs.

As always in my writing, theory is tempered with the fact that I have been there — I've brought up two kids with dozens of rescued problem dogs around, and they're fine, healthy, now 15 and 7 respectively, and without a single toothmark to show between them!

I'm not saying there haven't been moments — like the day my 3 year old calmly walked into a full blown dog fight between a Doberman and a German Shepherd in the park, telling them they were being "naughty doddies" — and they stopped and stared at him in astonishment, as did the horrified owners and I!; or the time I found little Stephen, aged 8 months, inside the indoor kennel, attempting to stuff a 4 week old miniature poodle puppy head first into his mouth.

However, that's really nothing compared to what they got up without dogs being involved, and I can sincerely and honestly say, everyone always got on splendidly.

I wish you as much fun with your dog and your baby as I have had over the years with mine.

With all my best wishes to you and lots of love.

— *Silvia Hartmann-Kent, September 1996*
— *Third Revised Edition 1998*

It's good for your dog to know that...
at least SOME things never change!

CHAPTER 1
HANDLING

Pregnancy, child birth and the reality of living with a baby 24 hours a day are among those events you must have experienced for yourself in order to understand what they are really like. However, your main task in preparing your family dog for the new arrival is to start to think ahead about the possible pitfalls.

Begin to imagine the demands that will be made on your dog and take steps well in advance, identifying and anticipating possible problem areas so they need never arise.

This is what this book is all about — preventing problems.

I also hope that it will answer the questions which tend to be raised when a new addition to the family is on the way. Do remember, most dogs adapt very happily to life in the new extended family and statistically, only a minute percentage ever need specialist advice.

I hope you will find as you go through the sections that your own dog is already perfectly well prepared. If you are unsure, there is a quick Check List in Appendix II to help you put your mind at rest.

Should you already have a problem, I hope you will find some guidelines towards a solution.

All training methods offered are simple and do not involve physical or mental confrontation. Should you need further advice or help, look at Further Information in Appendix IV.

Let us now begin by looking at an aspect of dog ownership which every member of the family will be involved in on a daily basis and that is very important for dogs, and babies.

Handling

Handling is about how a dog reacts to being touched by people he knows, be it during simple care taking activities such as grooming, bathing etc., during training, or simply as stroking or petting.

Peter and Julie were very concerned that their 3 year old Collie Luke might bite their toddler, as the dog hated having his back end touched and would snap if anyone reached for his rear or his tail.

Young babies and toddlers grab at just about anything. We all know that. They also try to pull just about anything into their mouths and suck or bite them.

It follows that it is most important for the family dog to be happy about being touched and handled all over his body and also to have his tail, ears and hair lightly pulled.

Even dogs that do not snap or react badly to being handled will benefit from the 'handling action plan', because

a. dogs really enjoy it;

b. it is relaxing for the owner;

c. it helps towards bonding;

d. it makes every day tasks such as bathing, treatments or grooming easier;

e. potential troubles such as fleas, grazes etc. are detected before they can cause problems.

As with all the "action plans" that are still to come, you do not have to make a great effort or spend inordinate amounts of time to teach your dog. All it takes is just a few minutes a couple of times a day to make real progress in no time at all.

Handling — Basic Principle

Teaching your dog to enjoy being touched is in no way meant to be a struggle. **Take your time** — there is nothing to be gained by trying to rush through the steps of the action plan; remember that **this is a trust building exercise** and that you want your dog to be absolutely reliable in the end. Should your dog fail to cooperate perfectly at first, don't get upset or angry — just walk away and try again later when you've both calmed down.

Handling — Action Plan

1. Find a time when your dog is naturally relaxed — after a walk or after a meal. Simply **stroke his head and shoulders with firm, long, slow strokes and talk quietly** to him. Do this until he is relaxed and happy and accepts it quietly, without becoming excited or playful. This stage can take anything up to two weeks of twice daily sessions depending on your dog, but it is important to take your time, as this exercise lays the foundations for all that follows.

2. Only when he is happy with the above, **sit on the floor with him**. Extend the strokes, still starting from his head and shoulders, to his back and towards his chest. Do not at this stage push on too quickly, remember we are trying to build his confidence.

3. Very gradually, over a period of 10-20 sessions if necessary, **extend the stroking area**, until you can stroke every part of his body without him becoming unhappy, overly playful or tense.

4. Only then **move on to lightly holding his ears, paws and tail** — only a touch at first, with a little more pressure each time you do this exercise. Should your dog show resentment or fear, back off and go back to the safe areas for a time.

5. Only when you can hold every part of his body quite firmly, **start gently tugging his fur a little** — and I mean gently! Build this up again until your dog shows no fear or resentment, keeping little grabby hands that don't yet know their own strength in mind at all times.

6. The last stage is to **ask other people your dog knows well to pet and stroke him** as often as possible.

You yourself should continue to do at least one handling session, no matter how brief, at least once a day. Once your baby has arrived, those few intimate minutes with your dog will not be affected by your state of fitness and will serve to establish continuity in a world which, for both you and your dog, has probably been turned upside down.

Chapter 2
EXERCISE

If you are pregnant for the first time, it is hard to look beyond the actual birth — the major event looming ahead. Furthermore, not many women really realize that even the easiest of births will make walking difficult, if not impossible, during the first two weeks at least.

This is partially due to discomfort and partially due to bleeding which occurs naturally after each birth but which does require you to rest in order to facilitate proper healing.

Susan sought help because her 18 month old Labrador Lady had become very destructive around the home and in the garden since the birth of the baby. After talking for a while it transpired that Lady had been used to going for very long walks all through Susan's pregnancy.

As Susan had a number of stitches, she found walking now very uncomfortable and had not taken Lady out at all since the baby had been born. Lady was now exercised only briefly by the husband when he came home from work.

Even when you have fully recovered from child birth there will be further impediments to the long, leisurely walks and fun and games with your dog in the park that your dog might have been accustomed to enjoying with you.

Sheba, a German Shepherd female, had developed a whole catalogue of problems during the last year... continuous barking, stealing articles and refusing to give them up, not coming in from the garden when called and over-excitable behavior with visitors were among them.

Sheba was hardly exercised at all as Mary just could not cope with the dog pulling on the lead and the baby walker at the same time. When Mary went out, Sheba had to stay at home.

Exercise does not, however, simply consist of walking the legs off your dog.

Dogs enjoy going out not only because they like walking, but also because of the sights, the sounds, the smells and the excitement and expectation of what and whom they are going to meet.

It is a fact that there are dogs who hardly ever leave their owner's house, and yet live contented and happy lives, because they are provided with interest and mental stimulation in other ways.

Talking to, or playing with your dog, grooming or training him, can all provide interest in a dog's life if walks are in short supply.

One of the very best ways to make a dog's life interesting is to involve the dog as much as possible in all the activities of the family — be it going out to a picnic on Sundays, to going the high street shopping, to visiting friends and relatives. To begin with, all these activities might require you to take the time to teach your dog patiently — on the lead and with many rewards — how to behave in such social situations. This is well worth doing, in my opinion, as the more you take your dog, the more he or she becomes accustomed to behaving well, and the end result is a dog that you can really take anywhere and who will be welcomed anywhere.

Later on, when your child is a little older, you can walk to schools together and to parks or go exploring "as a family". The more you can include your dog in whatever is going on, and the more inventive you can be to find tasks and simple things for your dog to do, the better your family life will be, and the better your relationship with the dog will become.

Exercise — Action Plan

1. Now's the time to **put well meaning friends and relatives to the test when they offer to take your dog out for you.** Try it for a week and see how much exercise your dog is really going to get if you cannot take him out yourself.

2. **Get your dog used to staying at home** on occasion, especially if you feel like walking a lot during your pregnancy.

3. Most importantly, **now's the time to teach your dog to walk on a loose lead**. Once your baby has arrived, this task will be one hundred percent more difficult. If you're unsure how to do this, you can find a brief outline in the 'Exercises' chapter.

4. **Exercise also includes keeping a dog's mind exercised.** Simple obedience exercises, tricks and games can all be employed to keep a dog happy and relaxed even when it does not go out for long walks every day. See 'Tricks and Games' in Appendix I for some ideas on the subject.

5. **Teach your dog to retrieve articles**. This will enable you to stay in one place while the dog does all the running and can be very useful to provide both physical exercise as well as mental stimulation indoors or in the back yard.

6. **Consider joining a dog training club**, even if your dog is very obedient already. You can find advertisements for classes on your veterinarian's notice board or in pet shop windows. Visit all the clubs in your area before you decide which one to join. Look for a club with a happy, quiet atmosphere, relaxed dogs and friendly instructors.

Going to classes together once a week can be a welcome break from your normal everyday routine for both you and your dog and it will be a chance to spend some quality time together again without any distractions.

Chapter 3
FOOD

Some dogs can take a pretty dim view of a toddler crawling towards their bowl while they are having their dinner, or having a favorite bone taken away and sucked. I remember a friend coming round for coffee once. We were chatting and then noticed that her 9 month old girl had gone very quiet. Understandably alarmed, we looked for her and found her under the coffee table, contentedly chewing on a very old and well worn marrow bone!

A large percentage of accidents can occur in situations involving food, so it is important that your dog should learn not to guard his bowl and bone, and to take food treats gently.

Food – Action Plan

1. **Feed your dog twice a day** to keep his blood sugar levels fairly evenly distributed. This will make your dog less likely to be starving hungry and much less likely to want to fight over food.

2. **Do not leave uneaten dog food lying around**. Get your dog used to eating his food straight away by putting the bowl down, setting an egg timer to five minutes and immediately removing the food when the time is up. Harden your heart and do not offer any further or alternative food until at least four hours later. This trick also works with children incidentally!

3. **Train your dog to be 'baby safe'**. The trick is to teach your dog that it is 'Good News' indeed when humans approach the bowl. Rather than marching up to the dog in a very aggressive manner and tearing the bowl from under its nose ('to teach it

who's boss'), wait until all the food has been eaten – then add a particularly tasty treat to the bowl.

Within a very short period of time your dog will be eating and looking at you at the same time, virtually willing you to put your hand in his bowl. You can then progress to picking the bowl off the ground before adding the treat, then giving it back.

4. **Ask friends and visitors to put the odd treat into your dog's bowl** at any time of day. If you can, have some visiting children do the same; they will enjoy this and so will your dog!

5. **Practice taking your dog's bone or chew away from him in the same positive way** as you taught him to enjoy your hand near his bowl. Exchange the bone/chew for a particularly tasty treat, then give it back straight away, praising your dog as you do so.

Some dogs have a tendency to revert to timber wolf mentality over bones, even if patiently taught. If you have a dog like that, it might be safer not to give any bones until your child is old enough to appreciate this particular facet of Fido's character – five or six, depending on the child.

6. **Teach your dog to take food treats nicely** and without snapping. This is best done in the evening after your dog's main meal to begin with. Sit in a chair, or on the floor with your dog and have a few small treats in one hand. The other hand can be used to push down gently on the top of the dog's nose if he or she should attempt to snap. Talk all through with your dog in a meaningful manner and say, "Take it nicely, that's a good dog!" rather than the negative and not instructional "NO". Treat this as a regular practice 'exercise' – your dog is bound to enjoy it.

7. **Teach him not to touch food unless you have specifically allowed him to do so.**

You will find this comes in handy when your baby starts

learning to eat food on his own while crawling on the floor! Place the biscuit on the floor in front of you and tell your dog to "leave it!!" To begin with, the help of a leash and a little volume and perseverance may be required before your dog understands.

Table Manners

You will, in due course, spend hours and hours, day in and day out, patiently teaching your child how to feed him or herself, first with fingerfoods, then with a spoon, then later on with knife and fork.

Teaching table manners to a dog, on the other hand, is laughably easy and quick by comparison as you'll find out!

1. Nowadays it is considered perfectly okay to feed a dog at the table, or to give bits of your food from your plate if, like most of the population, you have occasional dinners on your lap in front of the TV.

Whether or not you choose to do this is entirely up to you; **however, the dog should not be pestering**, and he or she should give you a respectable space of about 3 feet or so, only coming forward to take food if invited, and sitting or lying down again quietly while you are eating.

2. Alternatively, you might like to decide that your dog will remain in a certain place so you can eat in peace. This is very easily taught; just decide this is going to be the new rule, **mark out a spot with a blanket or towel, and ask your dog to lie on it**. At any time the dog gets up, quietly return it to the spot and give it a small food treat; at the end of the meal, give something special "because you've been so good" — even if at first you had to get up 20 times. Once again, with a little perseverance it doesn't take much more than ten days or so for the dog to have fully understood — and your baby will not have the experience of squealing with delight as doggy licks cereal off sticky fingers as soon as your back is turned.

3. **It is also nice to have your dog sitting quietly while you prepare his dinner, and to wait for you to invite him to eat it.**

To teach this is, divide your dog's food into five or six small portions. Prepare a portion, then put it back into the cupboard. Some time later, bring in the dog, ask it to sit, and do not hand over the bowl until he or she has complied.

Just one week and your dog will have great table manners.

Chapter 4
TOYS

Toys can and do cause a lot of problems. Up to the arrival of the baby the only toys around the house will have belonged to the dog, so it is only natural that he will assume all the baby's toys must belong to him as well.

The fact that the baby's toys will also lie on the floor and are usually made of similar materials does not of course help to lessen the dog's confusion.

Lastly, toys have in many instances replaced parts of prey animals and are like trophies in many a dog's mind, bringing out ancient and instinctive competitive behavior and guarding behavior — but only if the dog has not been taught the ways of the human world.

Micky, a Jack Russell Terrier, was in the doghouse for systematically shredding all baby Simon's toys. Simon's mother was getting worried because Micky would now growl at the eight month old boy and snatch toys from his hands.

His owners could not understand why Micky did this, as he had lots of toys of his own — in fact Micky's toy box was just as well stocked as Simon's.

To avoid toy problems, take the following steps.

Toys — Action Plan

1. **Limit the number of toys the dog can play** with to one or two favorite articles. There really is no need for more, unless your dog is a very young puppy and still teething — in which case prepare for tears at bed time when "favorite teddy" has lost his nose, eyes and limbs!

2. **Practice taking toys away from your dog.** This is easily done by exchanging the toy for a food treat and praising sincerely, then giving it back straight away.

Under no circumstances should you adopt an aggressive stance when you take a toy from your dog — your dog might let you get away with it, but he most certainly would not back down from a little baby. Remember you are trying to teach the dog to actually look forward to someone approaching him and his toy and to give him confidence that there's no need to guard his possessions.

3. **Buy some fairly cheap perfume** and use this as a marker for objects your dog is not allowed to touch.

A very light spraying with the perfume from a fair distance (a foot or more) is quite enough — the scent will stand out like a torch to a dog's sensitive nose; but please make sure you do not use perfume you would put upon yourself — this might lead to some major confusion for your dog!

An object to practice with could be a new furry toy or just a piece of cloth, for example. Use the command "leave it!!" (see also Food) as soon as your dog approaches the object.

Practice this when you are at ease and have time to see that the dog leaves the marked object alone. Start by placing it in a position where the dog is not likely to pick it up, then leaving it on chairs or low tables before finally moving it to the floor.

Remember to put the article away when you have finished the training session; if your dog gets hold of it and has a chance to play with it or chew it, the wrong lesson is learned!

4. Now is the time to **discourage anyone from "rough housing" with the dog.**

Late one evening, I received a hysterical phone call from Jenny. Her four year old labrador cross had grabbed her little 8 month old daughter Shelley by the arm and started to shake her like a rag doll. On further inspection in turned out that Jenny's husband had encouraged the dog ever since it had been a puppy to wrestle boisterously, had rolled about on the floor with it and had taught it to grab on to his arm and growl — just "like a police dog" ...

As this isn't a book about puppy training, it is obviously too late to be telling anyone that such rough and aggressive play encourages all the wrong instincts in a pet dog and can teach the dog many dangerous lessons which could lead to a lot of very serious problems later on in life — as it obviously did in the case of Jenny and Shelley.

Still, dogs do learn new things and can continue to learn to change their minds about behaviors, right up to the dying day, providing the new rules are made perfectly clear and strictly adhered to.

Aggressive play — where the dog growls, gets overexcited, starts to snap or bite onto clothes or shoes, or playing tug-of-war with an article or toy — **must be stopped** when there are small children around, and replaced with other, more controlled kinds of play activity, such as retrieving a ball or Frisbee.

A dog can not be expected to understand that one behavior

is okay and is actively encouraged with one kind of person, but might well lead to the death penalty when engaged in with another type — in the case above, who was in the end really responsible for the damage and the trauma experienced by little Shelley?

5. Check all areas to do with toys and playing for instances of "hyperactive over-excitement" and begin right away to **retrain a more balanced attitude.**

> *Poppy, a cross breed, was crazy about squeaky toys. The slightest squeak would send her barking, jumping and generally going crazy with excitement.*
>
> *Her owner Pat was at her wit's end and worried that Poppy would inadvertently hurt the baby, as there were squeaks in little Daniel's play-gym, his Activity Bear, his shape sorter, his teddy and even in some of his rattles.*

It is very common for dogs to take a particular sound as an excuse to go wild with excitement. The rattle of car keys, the sound of the leash being moved, the ringing of the telephone, the sound of the door bell, a squeaky toy (as in Poppy's case) and a whole host of others.

The owner's natural reaction to this is to try and avoid making the particular sound in order to stop the dog from becoming over-excited. But this approach is not a cure and usually serves to make the problem worse and worse.

All of the sounds above have in common that they only occur just before something exciting is going to take place — a game, a walk, the arrival of a visitor, mum dropping everything and rushing headlong for the telephone etc.

These sort of problems can be cured quite simply by making

the sounds randomly a number of times — but without anything happening at all. In Poppy's case her owner was advised to squeak the toy frequently off and on throughout the day while telling the dog clearly at the same time, "It's just a sound, it doesn't mean anything."

Initially Poppy went mad with excitement each time but she soon calmed down and lost interest in the sound, only becoming excited about the toy when she was actually allowed to play with it — and little Daniel could at last play with his Activity Center in peace.

Chapter 5
SLEEPING PLACES

Beds, baskets, hidey holes and sleeping places in general can cause problems, especially when a dog feels the need to protect them from the human members of his family.

Unfortunately, dogs and babies tend to find the same kind of enclosed spaces attractive, which can make the situation worse.

Ria, a small Terrier Cross, was very tolerant of the three young children in the household — but not when she had taken up residence under the coffee table in the sitting room.

Ria would snarl and snap at anything that tried to enter her 'den' and her owner Cindy was getting increasingly concerned about her possibly biting one of the children who seemed to make a beeline for the table and Ria every time her back was turned.

Every dog deserves a 'safe place' to which it can retire when the going gets rough — preferably in a quiet room not accessible to the child or children.

Such a 'safe place" is not only good for the dog, but can also be a real help to the owners as well as it is often much less stressful for everyone concerned to send the dog to his bed rather than to have to command and reprimand the dog over and over again.

An indoor kennel or a crate (the civilized word for a cage) can provide an ideal retreat for your dog. Dogs usually enjoy staying in this kind of 'den' providing they have been taught initially that it is a good place to be (see 'Crate Training in Appendix I).

However, a family dog must not feel the need to protect his sleeping places from familiar human beings — with young babies or toddlers around, this could lead to very unpleasant situations.

General Principles

As before, **do not take an aggressive stance when trying to train a dog who guards his or her sleeping places.**

Aggression always breeds aggression, and although you as an adult might force the dog into submission, it will not stand for such treatment from the baby.

Teach the dog to think that if someone approaches his sleeping place he can anticipate good things happening to him, as opposed to cringing back in anticipation of a fight or a struggle.

Sleeping Places — Action Plan

1. **Set up a 'safe place' for your dog** and get him used to going to it and staying in it (see 'Go To Bed!' and 'Crate Training' in Appendix I).

2. If your dog likes to 'guard' special places such as behind the sofa, under a table, in a favorite chair for example, block off, remove or **fill in these trouble spots for time being** until your dog has become accustomed to using his new retreat instead.

3. **Approach your dog in his new retreat in a friendly manner,** stroke and pat him, praise him and give him an occasional treat.

Should your dog be very much on guard and growl at you if you get too close, you could start by keeping a safe distance to begin with and to roll food treats towards him. Slowly decrease the distance until you are near enough to begin the above.

4. **On occasion sit or stand on your dog's bed** — and watch for the look of sheer amazement on your dog's face when you do this for the first time!

Invite him to join you and have a cuddle; this way your dog will feel quite relaxed when your baby eventually discovers the joys of crawling into the dog's basket.

Sleeping Arrangements

One question you should also ask yourself is: where does my dog sleep at the moment, and do I intend to change this once the baby has been born?

Gerry, a Spaniel, had started to mess in the house. He was five years old and had been perfectly house trained before the birth of the baby. When I asked about sleeping arrangements, it turned out that Gerry had slept in the bedroom right up until the baby had arrived. He now slept in the kitchen and was no longer allowed upstairs at all. He was not allowed in the dining room any more and the furniture in the sitting room had also become out of bounds to him.

While we were talking he tried to climb onto the sofa and was pushed off by his owner with the words, 'Get off! Baby doesn't want your horrible dirty hairs all over her settee!'.

If your dog sleeps with you in the bedroom or on the bed and you do not wish to continue with this arrangement once the baby has been born, be sure to make all the necessary changes well in advance. The same applies to the question whether or not the dog is allowed on the furniture.

This is purely a matter of personal preference and only you can decide one way or the other, but **the point is to be aware of how your dog will feel**.

There will be many changes in your household due to the baby and for your dog this can be very frightening indeed. Dogs need routines because they give them a feeling of security and of what to expect next in the bewildering world in which we humans live.

Changing a dog's routine sleeping place is an important issue to him and should therefore be firmly resolved while everything else is still comparatively normal.

Getting your dog accustomed to his new routine in advance will make life easier for you too, as this will mean one little thing less on your mind.

Most importantly however, your dog will then not be able to connect the new routine with the arrival of the baby in any way.

Chapter 6
JEALOUSY and ATTENTION

With the best will in the world, your dog will not receive the same amount of attention from you after the baby has been born. Most dogs adapt to this change, but the transition can be made much smoother by a little foresight.

If you've never had a baby before, it comes as a shock to discover just how much time it will take up — every bit there is and sometimes more. In fact, women are biologically programmed to have the baby on their mind continuously, at least for the vital first few months.

Think about it. Even if your baby behaves strictly according to schedule — and only about one in every hundred do — you will have to feed, burp, wash, change, dress and rock him or her to sleep every four hours. And when you're not directly engaged in these routine care taking activities, you'll still be wanting some time just to hold, explore, look at and cuddle your baby. And when he or she finally gone to sleep, you'll be looking in every so often to check on her well being.

Even that is not all. Friends and relatives will be visiting to see the baby; midwives and health visitors will be popping in and out; there's all the extra house work the baby inevitably creates on top of the work you normally do; you might want to give extra attention to your spouse so that he doesn't feel left out.

Add to this that you most certainly won't feel very energetic at the time it becomes very obvious that a different world has arrived for your dog right out of the blue.

Your main concern therefore must be to **lessen the difference between the 'before' and 'after'** to some extent.

Attention — Action Plan

Before The Birth

1. **Avoid focusing too much of your loving energy on your pet dog**, especially towards the latter stages of pregnancy, when time can seem to pass excruciatingly slowly. For your dog's sake, find someone else to talk to on occasion or leave him behind when you go out.

2. **Teach your dog that there could be times when he is not required.** To test his response, sit on the sofa, cuddle a cushion and talk lovingly to it.

Will he try to push in, claw at you, bring toys to get your attention? Now's the time to teach him so when the baby arrives, he can't blame it for the sudden change in your behavior. Tell him many times, out loud, that you love him as much as ever, and that just because you're busy with something else for a little while, doesn't mean you've stopped caring about him.

3. If you are always the one to feed, groom, train and exercise your dog, **get someone else to do these things for you on occasion**. This will prepare your dog for the time you might have to spend in hospital, and on your return home, when you're not yet as mobile.

4. Generally **prepare your dog for the possibility of an overall (albeit temporary) lack of attention**. Examples of this would include to change your dog's diet temporarily to a canned or dried product if you usually cook elaborate meals for him, to have his fur cut short to eliminate the need for daily grooming, or to gradually reduce the length and frequency of walks and outings.

5. **Be on the lookout for any current behaviors** by your dog that might be all right and bearable now, but might lead to "negative attention" once the baby has arrived, and take any training action that might be necessary.

Just pretend that there's a baby on the floor in the middle of the sitting room, or that there's a baby sleeping fitfully upstairs, for example, and you will begin to get an idea of what I mean.

Sit down now and make a list of all the behaviors — from jumping up when greeting, to barking when playing, from pulling on the lead to growling over the food bowl, from not coming right away when called in from the garden to whatever your dog might be doing that isn't a problem while you've got the time and nerves left to deal with it, and remedy these now. You will be doing everyone a massive favor.

After the birth:

The First Meeting

It is quite possible you will feel a little apprehensive and less than entirely relaxed and confident when your dog first meets your new baby. You might wonder if your dog will like the baby.

Dogs on the whole have no opinion at all about the baby yet — but **they will be watching you for clues what opinion they ought to have.** If you are nervous and tense, the dog is likely to be the same and might become suspicious of that strange new creature on your lap.

Ideally, be cheerful and loving towards the dog and let it have a good sniff.

Most dogs will not actually lick the baby, just put their noses very close without touching. If the dog should lick the baby, don't worry, it is not be the end of the world (see 'Hygiene'); further, many dogs might need to taste things for a real in depth examination — they have a special scent/taste organ in the roof of their mouths.

Talking about sniffing — a word about nappies (diapers) at this point and their contents. Dogs the world over are absolutely fascinated with smelly objects, and many, many dogs have gotten themselves into big trouble and onto the last train to the vet's table by jumping into a pram (carriage) or onto a sleeping baby and pulling on the nappy — you can imagine what the horrified parents thought they were going to do!

I think probably the best way forward is to show a nappy to the dog, let it sniff it, and then tell the dog to "leave it!!" (see also Food and Toys). This should satisfy the dog's curiosity — but I would still advise you to keep bins with used diapers high up and out of reach ...

If you are worried that your dog might jump on the baby, place the baby in someone else's arms or on the sofa and kneel by your dog's side, holding the collar firmly but gently.

Say things like: 'This is my own puppy, do you like it? Doesn't it look funny?", etc. etc. Your voice will automatically become soft and loving as you talk about the baby and to your dog this will sound like praise — the ideal setting.

This also works the other way around; when you are holding the baby, talk to the baby about the dog: "Look baby, here is Fido. He is a good dog. He's going to help me look after you." etc. etc. Again your dog is experiencing loving words in the baby's presence which is an excellent start to their future relationship.

If your dog shows no interest in the baby at all and looks away or just pays attention to you instead, still proceed as above and talk to him in a loving way about the baby.

It is vital at this early stage that your dog should learn to think along the lines of 'When this new creature is around, there is a lot of love for me as well. Therefore I like having it around.'

The First Few Weeks

Bruno, a Doberman, had been all right with the baby at first. Now, four weeks later, he was beginning to show signs of aggression towards the baby, giving it 'dirty looks' as the husband termed it, and growling at it when he was close by.

When I saw this family, there was an air of great strain and unhappiness about them, both husband and wife repeatedly shouting at the dog and pushing him away harshly when he got too close to the baby. Eventually, the wife took the baby away. As soon as they had left the room, the husband relaxed visibly, starting to stroke the dog and to talk soothingly to him.

As far as Bruno was concerned, it could always be like this — if only he could get rid of the baby...

Jealousy — Action Plan

1. **Avoid shouting, pushing, smacking or hitting your dog when the baby is near at all cost** — just remember what Bruno thought of that in the example above. Use only positive instructions such as 'Sit' or 'Down' rather than negative commands such as 'Leave' or 'Off' so your dog knows what you want him to do and you can praise him for obeying. If your dog is very boisterous and won't leave you or your baby alone you can attach a length of line to the dog's collar and tie it up close to you. A small dog can be controlled in this way by wrapping a lead around your foot. Both these methods control the dog's behavior effectively — but without you personally becoming unpleasant towards the dog.

As a last resort, go for a "time out" — asking the dog to go to bed or to taking him to stay in his crate for a while.

2. **Do not fall into the trap** of 'trying to make it up to the

dog' by giving him a lot of extra attention (i.e. fussing over him or playing with him) when the baby has gone to bed. This will be interpreted by the dog — just as Bruno did in the last example — like this: "When the baby is here, they ignore me. When it is not here, I'm having a wonderful time. Therefore I don't like the baby."

Ideally you should sometimes pay attention to the dog when the baby is present, and sometimes ignore him when the baby is not present.

> *Ken, an elderly gentleman, rang me, very upset. His nine year old companion Moss, a Border Collie, was barking continuously whenever his daughter came to visit with the baby — his first grandson. They had tried all kinds of things to "shut him up", but nothing had worked.*
>
> *Now the daughter was threatening not to visit ever again, unless he got rid of the dog.*

If you have a jealousy problem already, make a real point of being pleasant and attentive towards the dog when the baby is around (even asleep in a push chair will do).

In the case above, the problem was solved very simply by Ken spending the first ten minutes of each visit giving Moss some tasty treats and reassuring his companion that he had not stopped caring about him. Moss settled a little quicker each time, and now looks forward to the visits, because for him, baby means extra attention and extra treats.

3. **Make a point of praising your dog occasionally when he's doing nothing in particular,** sleeping in his basket or amusing himself quietly on his own, for example.

It often happens that a dog will only receive attention when he's being 'naughty' if his owners are busy or preoccupied — and you will be both just after the birth of your baby. The result is of course that the dog will be 'naughty' more and more often to remind you of his existence.

A quick pat or a cuddle and a few kind words to your dog at the right time is an easy way of reassuring him that you have not forgotten him and to avoid attention related behavior problems.

Kim, a Samoyed, was driving her owner Michelle to distraction by barking, rushing around and a number of other activities when Michelle tried to breast feed the baby.

Orders and commands would not stop her and when Michelle tried shutting Kim in the kitchen she howled like a wolf and scratched madly at the door — which made feeding times extremely stressful for Michelle.

Be aware of 'attention seeking behavior' by the dog because it can take all kinds of bizarre forms.

Favorites are barking, whining, scratching at the door to be let out into the garden, picking up an object and challenging you to a 'catch me if you can' session but there are countless others — chasing shadows, chasing the tail, snapping at imaginary flies, pretending a visitor has arrived; the list is really quite endless and only limited by a dog's ingenuity.

If you try to punish this kind of behavior by shouting at your dog, telling him to stop, chasing him etc. you have in fact rewarded him, because he managed to gain your attention, which is what he wanted in the first place.

As far as a dog is concerned, negative attention (what we might think of as punishment) is much, much better than no attention at all. Some dogs will even go so far as to prefer a beating to being ignored.

Therefore, if you try and ignore such behavior, the dog will escalate in his efforts to make you 'sit up and take notice' — which is precisely what had happened in Michelle's case.

The best way therefore to cure problems relating to this and more importantly, to curb them before they get out of hand, is to reassure the dog that he or she is still loved as much as ever.

'Attention-seeking' is nothing more than 'love seeking'; a request to take notice, an attempt to make sure that one isn't forgotten, and that the other person still cares. Jealousy arises when one individual starts to feel unloved — and that's the same for dogs as it is for people.

Therefore, when the dog comes for attention in the first instance, and long, long before he has felt the need to employ such desperate measures to get through to the owner as in Michelle's and Kim's case, all that is needed are a few kind words, a smile, a pat on the head — a little attention at the right time, 'a stitch in time saves nine' indeed.

This is not always as easy as it sounds when you have so much else to think about, but in the long run, it's the only approach that will really work, and it will save you and your dog from any possible disruption and unpleasantness.

Dogs Who "Don't Like Children"

Every so often, I come across a case where the resident dog appears not to like children — he or she may growl, bark or snap when they see strange children out and about, and the dog may have had some bad experiences with children in the past.

It was, the owners admitted, a kind of last ditch effort to come and see me. Surely there was nothing to be done with Susie, a ten year old Jack Russell female who had hated children all her life and had actually bitten children on a number of occasions when she was younger.

Now there was a little granddaughter, and Susie would have to be put to sleep — or was there something else that could be done?

I will tell you a tale from my own experience with such dogs — whether anyone eventually decides to take the risk and give the dog a fair chance must be their own decision, because if it goes wrong, it will have been their responsibility.

Having said that, I once acquired a serious problem dog — a terrier cross collie bitch named Tara — who, indeed, hated children. To make matters worse, my own 18 month old son Stephen was (to put it mildly) a live wire and entirely lacked the common sense and sensitivity my older son had always exhibited when dealing with animals of any kind. In spite of dire warnings from just about everyone, I decided to give it a go.

Firstly, they were never left unobserved for so much as a second — if I was busy, one or the other of the pair was locked away securely.

Then, I began a "Stephen is wonderful" program by getting him to put Tara's food bowl down, giving her a small share of whatever food he was having, only playing with her when Stephen was around — all the while keeping her on the lead and a very watchful eye on the both of them.

It took a couple of months until they were the best of friends. Tara must have somehow taken Stephen out of the 'children' category, because she still isn't entirely reliable with any other children — but boy does she love him!

To this day — he's nearly ten now and she must be 15 — they still share crisps and cuddles on the sofa, and Tara accompanies Stephen as a highly reliable guard when he goes to visit the grandparents who live a few blocks away.

Chapter 7
HYGIENE

Hygiene is an interesting and emotionally charged area as opinions are deeply divided among experts on how much of a health hazard dogs really are, depending on which side of the fence they're on.

On the whole, people who do not own dogs will advise you that there are enormous risks in mixing dogs and babies. Experts who are dog owners themselves, on the other hand, believe that the risks are minimal, providing some fairly basic rules of hygiene are observed.

Try to find a health visitor or midwife who either likes dogs, or actually owns one, if you want to discuss the subject in more detail. Alternatively, talk to your veterinarian who may be the ultimate expert on 'dog-borne diseases'.

Please note that all the points in this chapter apply to normal, healthy children. Should your baby be premature or ill, you might have to take stricter precautions. Discuss this with any of the above, if necessary.

General Points On Hygiene

As far as transmitting disease or illness is concerned, the basic rule is: **the cleaner and healthier the dog, the smaller the risk**.

Most diseases transmitted by dogs to humans are caused by parasites such as worms (like the much publicized Toxocara Canis) or fleas or mites, which means if your dog does not have any worms, fleas or mites, it cannot transmit said diseases.

Dog hair is unsightly but unless ingested in large quantities is unlikely to cause any degree of harm to a healthy baby.

Dog saliva does carry large amounts of bacteria; for this reason it is vital that saliva should not get into open wounds. Any dog bite even if inflicted accidentally while playing should be cleaned professionally at your local hospital to avoid long lasting and painful infection. Normal healthy skin, however, will not suffer from occasional contact with it.

Any doggy 'accidents' (or baby accidents, for that matter!) in the house should be cleaned and disinfected with special materials available from your veterinarian, as these are both stronger and longer lasting than those available from your supermarket or pet shop.

This rule can be relaxed once your child is old enough not to crawl on the floor anymore and put everything they can get hold of into his or her mouth.

Hygiene — Action Plan

1. **Start worming your dog at 4 monthly intervals before the baby is born and continue to do so regularly afterwards**. Please make sure you enter the dates when you should be worming your dog in your diary and get an ample supply of tablets from your veterinarian; it is only too easy to forget if you are busy.

Your vet will advise you on what kind of medication and the dosage you need for your dog,

2. **Make an effort to get rid of fleas**. Fleas can carry diseases which could be introduced directly into the baby's blood stream; you will have to treat not only the dog but also his bedding and your carpets, too. In the United Kingdom some councils provide

a service to fumigate your house free of charge. Contact your local Town Hall and speak to the Department of Environmental Health, if you feel this to be necessary.

As before, your veterinarian will be able to supply you with remedies which are more powerful than those available elsewhere.

For preventing reinfestation you might consider a flea collar and a carpet freshner cum-insecticide can also be of use but watch out for a possibility of allergic reactions to these from any human or animal members of your household.

3. **Keep your dog clean and consider having his fur cut short** by a professional groomer before the baby is born. Don't worry how it looks; it will save you a lot of time to begin with and you can soon go back to the more glamorous (and more labor intensive) hair style when the baby is a little older.

4. **Make sure your dog has been inoculated**, using either standard inoculations or homeopathic nosodes. One of the diseases your dog will be protected against can be transmitted to humans (Leptospirosis or Weil's Disease) and although very rare, can be fatal.

However, do not have your dog inoculated during a time when your baby is just about to arrive or if your baby is ill, as in a few cases the inoculation itself can actually cause the disease to appear.

5. **Be sensible and do not use the baby's dishes for dog food and vice versa.**

6. **Keep some antiseptic soap around for washing your hands** after cleaning up after your dog (or baby), feeding him or after bathing him when he's rolled in something objectionable.

On the whole, however, trying to wash your hands every time you've touched the dog or anything that has been touched by the dog will probably drive you mad if he lives in the house with you. It is not essential unless you, your dog or your baby are ill. Discuss this further with your veterinarian, if necessary.

7. If your feed fresh or frozen meats intended for animal consumption be careful where you store them and **keep all implements used strictly apart** from your other kitchenware. Always scrub your hands thoroughly after handling them.

Proprietary canned, dried or semi moist dog foods on the other hand have been cooked and sterilized at great length and do not pose a health hazard any more than an ordinary can of beef stew unless allowed to go 'off'. While we're on the subject, eating dry dog food and dog biscuits has had no harmful repercussions that I'm aware of, although I wouldn't make it a habit!

8. Now would be a good time to teach your dog to "go" in a specific area in the garden or back yard — in a year's time that empty grass and patio are going to be covered by a child's tractor, trike, sandpit, paddling pool, balls, and the like. Take your dog out and encourage him or her to perform in that special area, always praising when he or she 'goes'. Clean up this area regularly to keep it fresh.

Chapter 8
PHYSICAL SAFETY

When we talk about physical safety with regards to dogs, the first thing that springs to mind is injury through dog bites. With the recent media coverage one could be forgiven to think that 'attacks' by household pets on their owners and children are a commonplace occurrence.

Fortunately this is not so. For every reported incident there are literally hundreds of thousands of happy, well adjusted family dogs who never put a paw wrong. It is as well though to be aware of possibly dangerous situations and to take sensible precautions.

Accidental Biting

A recent survey shows that 93% of all reported incidents of bites (in the UK) relate to dogs who have never bitten anyone before.

What this simple statistic means is there are thousands of owners who, right up until 2 seconds before the actual incident, would have sworn blind that their dog was 'absolutely trustworthy'.

Now I love dogs dearly. I work with them and own a large number myself — but I would never describe any dog as absolutely trustworthy. What does 'trustworthy' actually mean?

Carry, a seven year old mongrel, had bitten 18 month old Jason in the shoulder. The little boy needed over thirty stitches and as he was being treated in the hospital, the dog was taken to be destroyed. When the veterinary assistant was about to remove the body from the table, she noticed something in the dog's ear. It was a pencil stub that had penetrated Carry's ear drum.

A dog might be thoroughly good natured and 'trustworthy' around children, but **unsupervised children should never, ever be trusted around a dog**. Take heed, be aware of your responsibilities to your child and your dog and take some common sense precautions.

General Safety — Action Plan

1. **Invest in a sturdy playpen** while your baby is still very small. The wooden 'cage' type is the best, but if your dog is small, you might have to get the 'lobster pot' type to prevent him from getting in through the bars.

A play pen is a must for every mother, let alone dog owners, to ensure the child's (and the dog's!) safety when you have to leave the room to answer the telephone or the door, make coffee etc.

2. **Later on, safety gates can be used** to separate more active children from the dog when you are not in the same room to supervise. Buy the type that have a little door in them because we do not want to encourage the dog to jump the safety gates.

3. **Set up a retreat for your dog in a quiet place preferably not accessible to the child**. This can be a real life saver when you have visitors with children, during birthday parties or simply when you are too busy to supervise.

Note the word is 'retreat' and not 'solitary confinement'; get the dog used to the place (such as an indoor kennel, crate or basket) very gradually, until he actively looks forward to staying in it. See also 'Sleeping Places', 'Crate Training' and 'Go to Bed' for further information.

If at all possible the dog should be used to going to his retreat before the birth, so he does not connect being sent away by you with the arrival of the baby. See also 'Jealousy and Attention'.

4. **Keep an eye on your dog's general state of health at all times.** Physical problems leading to sore or sensitive areas are the most common reason for a dog biting or snapping when touched. A very common example of this is a dislike to be touched near the tail due to impacted anal glands; ear infections are often the reason for a dog reacting badly to be handled near his head or neck.

Non-Accidental Biting

A rather different situation arises when the dog bites not for immediate physical reasons, but when guarding or protecting his possessions, favorite sleeping places or his honor.

Khan, a Great Dane, had snapped at the young child in the family shortly after it had started to crawl. There had been no damage but his owners were shocked and deeply worried and were thinking of having him destroyed.

It transpired during the course of the interview that Khan had always guarded his toys, bed and bowl from both the husband and the wife ever since he had been a puppy.

Although Khan's owners described his 'attack' as surprising and shocking, all the signs had been there long before the baby ever arrived.

Khan was simply exercising his rights as a mature adult male to tell the baby off for encroaching on his possessions. He had also given all the warnings beforehand that would have been required from a normal, healthy dog when dealing with members of his own family.

The stages of a dog's warning are often overlooked and it is usually only with hindsight that the owners realize that the eventual bite was an inevitable escalation.

These are the stages of a dog's warning when dealing with family:

1. *The dog stops what he is doing and become very still.*

2. *If this is ignored, the dog will look threateningly directly at the intruder.*

3. *If the intruder still persists, the dog will flatten his ears and may growl.*

4. *Then he will lift his lip and growl more loudly.*

5. *Only then will the dog snap out, not to injure, but to teach the intruder a lesson.*

When a dog deals with puppies, one snap is usually enough to teach the pup to respect the other warnings. Human 'puppies' however, are not preprogrammed to understand this system and a dog will resort to going straight into the 'punishment' stage after his low level warnings have been repeatedly ignored.

There again, a snap that would only bruise a puppy through its thick skin and protective fur could seriously injure a human child.

Khan was not an aggressive or dangerous dog. His owners

had to make the choice whether they were going to retrain him or have him put to sleep — when all the problems could have been avoided with a little foresight.

Action Plan — Bite Prevention

1. **Look at your dog realistically and identify all possible problem areas**. Use the 'Check List' in Appendix II and answer the questions truthfully.

If you are even slightly unsure about any of the questions, refer to the related Action Plans and start practicing straight away, so your dog is safe before your baby arrives.

2. **Under no circumstance must you exhibit an aggressive 'me master, you dog' approach**. Your dog might well bow to your pressure under threat of punishment — but this is NOT going to make him safe with your baby.

Only by positive, reward based training as outlined in the 'Action Plans' can you ensure your dog will be happy to accept your little human near his toys, basket, bowl, etc.

Should you yourself have any problems like the above with your dog, now's the time to teach your dog the rules of human living, which are different from living in a pack of dogs. See Appendix IV for Further Information.

Male dogs in particular can often move into a kind of "protector" role with regards to female owners. This can be further exacerbated during pregnancy and while breast feeding by the abundance of female hormones in your system. The presence of these hormones can be picked up by a dog on your scent and the result is that in the dog's eyes you have become a 'super female' — to be loved and protected, but not necessarily to be obeyed!

If you have a serious problem, or if you are seriously

concerned, I strongly advise you to see an animal behavior counselor (see Appendix IV) for in depth assessment and personal help.

A serious warning:

Should anyone, no matter how expert he or she propounds to be, advise you to use methods based on physical punishment (such as hitting, shaking, choking, spraying unpleasant substances, using sound deterrents or shock collars), or psychological warfare (removing love, ignoring the dog, making his environment unpredictable/scary, or power games), thank them politely and show them the door immediately.

Methods based on physical punishment or psychological warfare are totally unsuitable for your situation and can be very dangerous indeed, especially when employed in the context of training a dog to be safe with babies and children.

General Safety

Injury to children can also occur as the result of a boisterous greeting, as an unsteady toddler can easily be knocked over; being caught accidentally by toenails is another common cause for injury. Safety in the car is another area you should be considering; as in all the other Action Plans, now's the time to teach the dog to behave in a civilized fashion to avoid causing accidents.

Action Plan

1. **Teach your dog to greet in a civilized manner** without jumping up. If you're not sure how to do this you can find some tips on the subject under 'Exercises' in Appendix I.

2. **Do discourage any jumping up**, anytime. Try to convince your partner or anyone else in regular contact with your dog of the necessity to do this with regards to your toddler-to-be.

3. **In the car some kind of restraint is a must** and you should fit a dog guard if at all possible. A dog leaping onto a baby in its carry cot or car seat can not only cause serious injury, but also distract the driver, thereby causing an accident. If you cannot fit a dog guard you might consider a nylon harness which acts as a seat belt for your dog instead. A cheaper way of restraining a dog in the car is to tie the dog, using a buckle collar (not a check chain, head collar or half check) and an extra lead, which is permanently attached to a strong point in the interior of the car. Start using it straight away to get the dog and yourself used to the procedure well in advance.

4. Run with your dog, waving your arms and shouting 'Yippee!' to **test how strong his chasing instincts are** (and take

no notice of what the neighbors might make of that!). Many dogs get very excited by this kind of behavior and react by jumping up, snapping at your ankles or trying to grab hold of you with their teeth. Should your dog react in this fashion, put him on a lead and teach him to run with you without jumping or snapping.

If your dog is very excitable, start with a slow jog and build it up gradually, talking to your dog in a meaningful way, telling him what to do, and praising him when he's getting it right.

Trust me, when your baby has become an active two year old, or brings little friends around to play, you will be glad you took the time.

Chapter 9
TRAINING YOUR BABY

So far we have only been concerned with 'child proofing' the dog. But as it usually takes two to tango, the child will also have to learn how to behave in an acceptable fashion towards the dog.

Sharon was seriously considering having her dog Elsa, a five year old Golden Retriever, put to sleep because the dog was apparently getting less and less tolerant of the two boys aged 2 and 4.

During the interview both boys smacked Elsa repeatedly, pulled her tail and ears, stood on her feet, threw toys at her and sat on her. None of this behavior elicited any comment from Sharon whatever. Finally Elsa growled as one of the boys tried to climb on her back.

Sharon jumped up in mid sentence, hit the dog around the face and dragged her from the room. On her return she said triumphantly, "Now do you see what problems I have?"

If things go wrong, it is often the dog who has to take all the blame.

Babies and young children are driven by the need to explore and cannot be expected to know or realize what consequences their actions might have.

Having said that, **it is never too early to point your baby in the right direction**, using — just as you did with your dog — encouragement and praise rather than shouting or punishment.

Training Your Baby — Action Plan

1. First and foremost, please **be realistic and do not expect too much of a small child** — they really have no idea of how other creatures feel and very little control over their strength or movements.

2. From a very early age, **hold your baby's hand and make him stroke the dog slowly and gently,** saying something like, 'Nice doggie, nice doggie' at the same time. Should the baby try to grab, straighten out his fingers for him and say something like, 'Like this, sweetheart. Nice doggie.'

3. When your baby gets a little older and can move about by himself, please **do not let him or her pester the dog.** Let him go up to your 'child proofed' dog by all means, but distract the baby away if you feel your dog has had enough. This is only fair to your canine companion and will start to build good habits for your baby.

4. If you follow this theme right from the start, you will never have 'the sort of problem' Sharon experienced in the last example. **Encourage friendly attention from your child towards the dog** within reason at all times. Should your child later try to behave in a way one could regard as unfair on the dog, tell him firmly that you are not happy and will not stand for this kind of behavior.

5. Encourage your child from a very early age to **take part in the every day care** of your family dog.

Even a very young child can 'help' with brushing, feeding, bathing and training the dog — you will find that both dogs and children love this and their relationship will benefit greatly.

Further, your child will learn an invaluable lesson — namely how to look after someone in your care properly, on an ongoing basis, and not just because it's a novelty that soon wears off.

Now, please go to Appendix II and complete the "Is my dog safe?" questionnaire.

Chapter 10
DECISIONS

You have read through the book and completed the 'Check List'. If you have found that your dog is well adjusted and perfectly happy, I hope your mind is now at rest and all is well in your household.

It would be unrealistic and naive to assume, however, that it is going to be the case for everyone.

Perhaps a dog is very old or ill. Perhaps it is a rescued dog with numerous problems in his past. Perhaps circumstances — where you live, whether you are well, financial problems — are against you. In these cases a decision will have to be made.

Should you keep your dog, and if not, what is to become of him?

I am often asked to advise whether a dog should be kept or not. **Neither I nor any other person can make this kind of decision for you.** All I can do is give you all the facts, for the final decision and the final responsibility lies with you alone.

Options

The very fact that you have gone to the trouble of buying and reading this book shows that you are a caring owner who shudders at the kind of mentality that makes some people simply dump a dog by the side of a highway.

If the decision has been made that it is not possible to keep the dog, there are basically two options available. You can either try to find a new home for your dog OR you can have him put to sleep.

Which one of these options you choose must depend on the dog and whether or not you believe that your dog would make a good pet for someone else.

Let us now look at both in more detail and see what they entail.

Finding A New Home

The 'big farm in the country' where a retired couple without children is going to look after the dog all day is what many people like to believe their dog will go to.

It is unfortunately a myth. Many, many more dogs are looking for homes than there are homes looking for dogs.

Even so, quite a number of 'second hand dogs' find new owners eventually. There are a number of organizations which might help you find a new home for your dog, or you could re-home your dog yourself.

Rescue Shelters

The most usual course of action is to take the dog to a rescue society such as the SPCA, or a local private shelter.

Although this is a possibility, please bear in mind that shelters are generally overcrowded and desperately short of funds; by taking your dog you will add to their burden. You must also be aware that it will mean you will be giving up all control over what is going to happen to the dog once you signed your name on the dotted line.

If you are going to give your dog up to a shelter, inquire first for how long they will keep the dog, as this can vary from a minimum of seven days up to however long it takes to find a new owner.

Breed Rescue Organizations

If your dog is a purebred dog, you might find there is a specialist rescue organizations just for your breed. These are often run locally and nationwide and are staffed by dedicated breed enthusiasts who can be most experienced and helpful.

Generally breed rescue organizations do not run kennels themselves and prefer the dog to stay with you until a new owner has been found although they will find somewhere for your dog to stay at short notice in an emergency.

Finding A New Home Yourself

If you have the time, this is probably the most satisfactory way of rehoming your dog. Begin by advertising in your local newspaper, placing cards in pet shop windows and news agent's notice boards. Dog training clubs, dog officers and veterinarians can also be of help.

Please be very truthful about any possible 'vices' your dog might have. If someone is put off by what he hears, he would not have been the right person for your dog in any case; and the dog would have been returned to you, perhaps even with some new problems added.

Get to know the prospective new owner; let the dog stay with them for a day, then a weekend before making the final move. This is much less traumatic to both you and your dog and the very best way to make a painful transition as easy as possible.

Euthanasia

Sometimes this can be the only option left to the owner and a more difficult and heartbreaking decision is hard to imagine.

In certain cases however it is the right decision and the only responsible thing to do.

Joan and her husband Larry were faced with this decision. Joan's dog Minnie, a poodle, was 16 years old and had been with Joan since she had been a child. Minnie was blind, nearly deaf and required a lot of special care as she also suffered from kidney failure.

"I took her to the surgery. It was the hardest thing I've ever had to do in my life. Looking back on it, I realize that I did the right thing. Minnie needed so much attention which I wouldn't have been able to give her and she would not have understood what was going on. Really, the arrival of the baby just forced me to make a decision I perhaps should have made a long time ago."

Your veterinarian will probably inquire into your reasons why you wish your dog to be put down and will be kind and sympathetic. You might be asked whether you wish to take the body home for burial or if you would like the vet to see to this or if you wish to have the body creamated.

It is best to make all the necessary arrangements, including paying the fee, well in advance. There is nothing more distressing than to receive a bill in the mail a week or so after the event.

You can stay with your dog if you like, or you can take him to the veterinary clinic and leave. The actual process is kind and totally pain free. The dog is injected intravenously with a concentrated barbiturate, which works so quickly that it is sometimes hard to believe the dog is indeed dead. He is literally put to sleep.

APPENDIX I
EXERCISES

Training Your Dog

In this section, I am going to go over a few basic ideas regarding dog training. If you would like to have more in depth advice on the subject, please refer to my book **"Training Your Dog With Love"** on dog obedience training, and Roy Hunter's **"Functional Dog Training"** on social training for the home.

Basic Principles

Whatever you want to teach your dog, be it simple obedience exercises or complex tricks, follow these basic rules:

1. **Think of yourself as an outstanding teacher** for your dog, rather than a concerned mum or dad. I assure you it helps!

2. **Be very clear what exactly you want your dog to do and how you are going to teach it** before you start.

3. **Always approach your training from a positive angle** and teach the dog what you want it to do, as opposed to trying to teach the dog to stop something or not to do something. Examples are teaching your dog to sit still rather than to try and teach it to 'stop jumping', teaching your dog to walk by your side rather than to try and teach it to 'stop pulling' etc.

4. Break each exercise into small and manageable components and **teach only one step at a time**. This makes

learning and teaching easier and it is how all professionals work and how television and film animals are taught.

5. **Never train your dog when you are not feeling well** and should you become angry or frustrated during a session, stop straight away.

6. **Always give your dog the benefit of the doubt** if he doesn't respond straight away. Try more or different types of training rather than resorting to punishment.

Walking Nicely On The Lead

This is one of the most important things for your dog to be able to do. A dog that walks nicely on the lead comes along when you're shopping, when you're going to take the children to school, goes out for walks, in short, is able to join in with all kinds of family activities.

If your dog doesn't do this perfectly yet, teach it now — once the baby has arrived, it will be much, much more complicated.

Action Plan

1. **Find a route that is reasonably safe**, reasonably distraction free, **and can be completed in ten minutes or less**. It could be just round the block, or up and down the lane — it doesn't matter if it's boring or if it has many distractions, as long as you get there as soon as you walk out of your house. This route will become your practice track for walking nicely on the lead.

2. **Put your dog on a lead that is at least 5 feet long**, and give it some line. In practice, this means that you loosen the lead right out so your dog cannot feel it anymore. (I do hope you've got hold of this book before you were in a position where the dog just

runs hell-bent for leather and doesn't care if you follow or not. If that's your problem, go to the special section for Steam Train Pullers instead). For your first attempt, the assignment is to get around your practice route with the lead being loose as much as possible.

• Yes, you're going to get tangled in the lead, wrapped round lamp posts or bushes, to begin with. And yes, you're going to learn the art of handling a lead in such a way that this doesn't happen anymore after a week of this.

• **use the lead to bring your dog back** if it's going somewhere inappropriate. Tell the dog over and over, "Stay on the sidewalk." Or, "Walk with me." After a week of this, your dog will know.

• **use the lead to make your dog sit** at road intersections, if there are any on your walk. Tell him about sitting because of the danger of traffic.

• **to begin with, be very flexible in your speed.** Stop for a while if your dog wants to sniff something, speed up a little when your dog picks up speed. The first commandment is to keep the lead loose.

• **to begin with, be flexible whether the dog's on your left, or on your right, or in front of you, or behind you.** As long as the lead's loose, and the dog's still moving in roughly the same direction, that's fine.

• **the only thing you should strongly object to is if your dog suddenly lunges into some direction or the other,** or hits the end of the long line sharply. Call your dog back and tell him or her right away that this is not on, that it could be dangerous for both of you, and that you're just going round the block (or up and down the lane).

Do this twice or three times a day for about a week. Once you feel that both of you have got the hang of the basics (i.e. you know how to handle the lead so it's loose all the time you're not actually using it to make an important correction, and how to encourage your dog not to lunge, to stay on the sidewalk and to sit at intersections, if any, and your dog has relaxed and learned that you just kind of walk this particular walk together), you can move on into the second stage:

• begin to **encourage the dog to be on the left or right side.**

• encourage the dog to **walk closely with you for a short period of time with full attention** (just a few steps close by your side with the lead completely slack is fine, then just let him wander along again).

• **take a break or do a bit of training** like Stay or Come.

Over a period of a month or so, lengthen the time you are actually requesting your dog to walk in the normal heel position by your side gently and steadily.

The instruction I use for this is "Walk closely." When the dog is in a close position by my left or right leg, depending on the circumstance, I look down and praise it gently while we're walking along: "Well, this is nice, isn't it? You and me, just meandering along the old lane ..."

Then, you can start varying your route and gradually introduce more distractions along the way, always making sure that you're asking no more of your dog in the way of understanding, good behavior and cooperation than your dog is ready to give you.

Walking On The Lead For Steam Train Pullers

Sometimes, you may have to retrain a rehomed or rescued dog that pulls no matter how long the lead is, and pulls flat out, like a steam train. For these dogs, we need a slightly modified approach.

Firstly, I would **recommend the use of a head collar**, such as the Halti™ , Gentle Leader™ or Figure Eight head collar.

Secondly, use the **very best food** you can find **to reward any attempt at cooperation**.

Thirdly, whatever "command" the dog has ever heard regards this activity must be firmly placed in the rubbish bin from now on, because it has by now become a signal to start pulling. **Use words that sound completely different** instead.

Fourthly, **use your practice track when your dog is as tired as possible**; i.e. just after a long walk. Another very useful tip is to walk it once, come inside, and straight out again — and again if necessary. It simply is impossible for a dog to sustain top levels of excitement over walking the practice track if it's done three times on the trot. If you are short on time, do a shorter practice track, but do it!

Walk the practice track at least three times, three times a day. If there's more than one of you in the household, do it each three times a day. Again, after a while the dog will relax on the practice track and the lead will be loose more than it will be tight. Once the dog is usually relaxed on the practice track, introduce all the methods from the section above.

Walking Nicely Everywhere

Once your dog is good on the practice track, begin to extend the length of the walks and the locations. Eventually, the dog will make the cross over and walk nicely everywhere.

To conclude this section, let me say that this is a very friendly, very easy way to train most dogs to walk with you in a civilized fashion in a relatively short period of time, providing you make an effort for a month or so to really teach your dog. If for whatever reason your dog begins to wander off or starts to pull later, go back to the old practice route to remind him/her of the original training.

Walking Nicely With A Pram (Stroller)

Getting your dog to walk nicely by the side of a pram or stroller is fairly easy providing the dog walks nicely with you in the first place. Teaching a dog to walk nicely and pushing a pram at the same time is virtually impossible. The dog ought to be taught separately and should have a chance to practice with you on his own before having to walk behind a pram, as outlined in the chapter before.

The correct position for your dog when you are pushing a pram is still by your side, not next to the pram, pushchair or stroller. In this position you will not take up the whole sidewalk and more importantly, you will not run over your dog's feet when you have to change direction suddenly.

A safety note: Never tie your dog's lead to your pram or stroller, either when walking or when parked outside a shop. This could be very dangerous if your dog is suddenly frightened or startled, or should decide to take off after a cat or another dog.

"Go To Bed!"

Sending a dog to his bed is a good way of preventing stress, trouble and strife, as it is much easier for both you and your dog to remove him or her from the scene, rather than to have to command and reprimand him constantly.

It is taught in four easy steps; how long your dog will take to learn this depends on his willingness to cooperate and on how much time you can invest in his training.

Step 1. Place some food in your dog's bed while he is watching. Take him back a few paces, holding his collar. Point to the bed, give a command (such as 'Basket!', 'Go to bed!' etc.) and let him go to eat the treat. Practice a number of times until your dog has become used to this 'game' and understands the basic idea.

Step 2. Still with a treat in the bed, send your dog to it from every room in the house. Practice until your dog does it happily and reliably every time.

Step 3. Stand by the bed holding the treat in your hand. Send your dog to the bed as before, but this time ask him to lie down in it. As soon as he is down, place the treat between his paws and praise at the same time. Practice until the dog automatically lies down when you give the 'Go to bed' instruction, rewarding and praising frequently.

Step 4. Gradually start moving away from the dog while he is lying down in his bed. Begin by moving only a step or two away and gradually extend the distance over a period of a week or two, until you can leave the room while the dog stays in his bed.

Practice this whenever possible. Sometimes reward the dog with a treat, sometimes with praise, but always reward him when he is in his bed, because this is what we want to encourage.

Should he get up before you have decided to end the exercise, simply and quietly put him back in the bed, leave him for a very short time, then let him come out if he wants to.

The important part of this exercise is not the length of time the dog spends in his bed, but whether you are in control of the situation. It takes a few months for a dog to learn to stay reliably for long stretches in his bed, so do not expect too much to begin with.

Crate Training

A crate, or portable dog cage, has a hundred and one uses.

It can provide a safe retreat for your dog in many situations, keep him out of harm's way, help with training problems, be used to transport him safely and provide a home from home for your dog when you're staying somewhere overnight.

A dog does not see a crate as a cage — "Oh dear I can't get out!" — but as a safe place — "What a relief, nobody can get in!" — providing he has been accustomed to staying in it gradually, and also providing the crate is used sensibly.

There are a few rescued dogs who have had bad experiences in the past with crates or cages and will never be happy to stay in one, but these are an exception; most dogs really enjoy the comfort and safety a crate can provide.

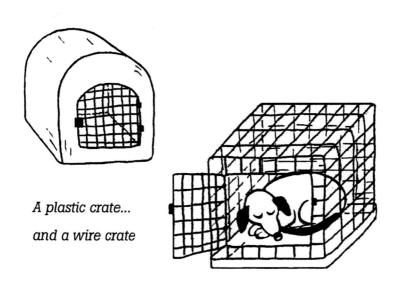

A plastic crate...

and a wire crate

Crate Training — Action Plan

Step 1. Leave the door open at all times. At feeding time, place the bowl into the crate. Hold your dog's collar, give a command such as 'In you go', 'Crate' etc., and allow your dog to enter the crate.

Step 2. After about a week of the above, proceed as before but shut the door when the dog is inside the crate.

As soon as the dog has finished his food, open the door to let him out.

Step 3. Place a chew, toy or bone in the crate. Using your usual command, let the dog enter the crate. Shut the door. Stay in sight and open the door after a few minutes — before the dog has become in any way unhappy or uncomfortable.

Step 4. Over a period of one or two weeks gradually lengthen the time the dog stays in the crate with the door shut. If you see him going into the crate voluntarily, remember to praise sincerely.

Step 5. Your dog is now crate trained. The crate should be available for your dog at all times and you can shut him in when and if this should be required.

Greeting Behavior

Why do dogs jump up at people? We all know the answer — dogs jump in order to get closer to people's faces. This is how a puppy would greet a returning adult dog, jumping up and licking his muzzle, both as a greeting and as a food begging behavior.

One of the nicest things about owning dogs is the sincere happiness they show when they greet us. This makes it doubly difficult for many owners as they feel it is wrong to punish the dog only because it is so happy to see them that it can't contain itself.

The reason why overexcitable greeting behavior is one of the most common complaints owners have about their dogs lies in a basic misunderstanding. Pushing an excited dog away and telling it off will lead to more displays of submission — i. e. more jumping up — rather than less.

Furthermore, as soon as you start to yell, push or shove, the dog will become stressed. In dogs this mostly manifests itself in even more excitable behavior, such as jumping up and down, barking, leaping, wriggling or even wetting in submissive urination.

General Points

Your dog needs to learn the differences between greeting other dogs and how people conduct their greeting with a dog.

The first instruction you will need to teach him is "Paws on the ground!"

If you remember, we said earlier that you should always give a positive instruction rather than a negative "Off" or "Down" because the dog needs to know what you want him to do, rather than what you don't want.

Also, as frantic greeting displays are often of a submissive nature, the calmer you can be, the better. A calm, quiet and very loving approach is the best long term remedy.

In order to be able to be calm in the first place, there is one basic dog training trick that you can use — if you cannot control your dog by voice, and your dog has not yet learned to control him or herself — take physical control, and that means having the dog on a leash or indoor lead (just a piece of rope or string permanently attached to the collar during the training period) will work.

Greeting Visitors

With visitors the very best method to achieve some measure of control over the dog is to put your dog on a longish lead before opening the door. If this happens a lot, you might be better off having an indoor line on your dog at all times — this avoids having to look for the lead and struggling to put it on when the door bell rings and the dog is already jumping around frantically.

Hold the end of the lead in one hand and stand on the rest, just near enough to the collar that your dog can stand up comfortably but cannot jump.

Pretend to be perfectly calm and relaxed, even if you have to struggle to keep him in place to begin with.

Open the door to your visitor, ask them to enter, and give them directions of where to go and to sit down. If your dog should lunge, bark or otherwise interrupt your dealings with the person outside the door, take a second to give your dog a pat and a quick, firm statement such as, "Thanks, but I'm dealing with this." You might also ask your dog to sit if you think it might help.

If the visitor enters, take your dog on the lead into the room once the visitor has sat down and begin a conversation, again remaining calm and centered, even if you are struggling to keep your dog under control. If your first attempt at this method is less than entirely easy and satisfactory, don't worry. This stage does not last long — just stick it out and very soon, I promise, your dog will start to learn and life will become much easier!

Talk to your dog in as friendly and firm a fashion as possible about the visitor (you can do this in "Stage Whisper" fashion, explaining to your visitor what's going on at the same time as relaxing and training your dog). Keep putting your full weight on the lead if necessary and stand or sit tight. With some dogs, it's a great help to have a pocketful of treats on you to help calm the dog, reward for good behavior, and persuade him or her that visitors are good news.

You will find that your dog will relax after a period of time. Depending on your dog, you may be able then let go of the lead and allow your dog to go to the visitor. Should your dog show any objectionable behavior, simply retrieve the lead and control the dog as before.

Within a week or so you will find that your dog has become accustomed to this new way of greeting visitors. You can then begin to wean him off the lead in stages, with the possibility of going back to more tighter control if your dog should have a relapse.

Weaning your dog off the lead works like this:

1. Hold the lead but don't stand on it.

2. Put the lead on but don't hold on to it.

3. Pretend to put the lead on.

4. Proceed without the lead.

The other alternative to training the dog, namely to lock it out in the garden, back yard or kitchen when visitors arrive, is not a good solution. Some dogs will learn to hate visitors because their arrival inevitably heralds a period of isolation, and in a dog's book there is no punishment worse than this, being a very companionable creature. Furthermore, the dog will not be able to guard you and your family if he is locked away when you answer the door.

So to train your dog, even if it seems a lot of trouble, is well worth doing, as a real effort for just a couple of weeks will result in a well behaved dog for his entire lifetime.

Greeting Family

As with visitors, the key is to lower the 'emotional temperature' of the greeting. This process begins already when you get ready to go out. Please do not indulge in excessive farewells. No matter how short or long your absence is going to be, always say goodbye to your dog in a friendly but offhand manner — "Going out now, Fido, but I'll be back soon. See you later." — and leave positively and happily.

If you come home by yourself, take some time to greet your dog quietly. With a small or young dog, it is best if you bend or kneel down to start with. Stroke and talk to your dog, saying pleasantly, "Paws on the ground, there's a good boy (or girl)", as soon as the dog prepares to jump up or claw at you. To begin with, you might need to make sure that the paws really are on the ground by putting a hand in the collar or standing on the indoor lead until it has begun to sink in!

If there's more than one person coming into your house on a regular basis, either teach them to do the same, or supervise and help them as much as possible.

Really impress the need for this kind of routine on every person living in your home; remind them that this is necessary because of the baby.

Some men are especially prone to spend ten minutes or so 'after a hard day at the office' roughhousing with the dog in the drive or entrance hall and for your training to be successful it is vital that this should be delayed until well after a civilized greeting has been established as routine.

Action Plan

1. **Say your 'goodbyes' briefly and cheerily** to avoid leaving your dog in a state of emotional turmoil.

2. **On your return, take your time to quietly pat your dog and speak with him or her calmly.** The ice cream in the shopping bag will last for another few minutes! If your dog goes absolutely crazy, leave the indoor line on his or her collar. Just stand on the lead and be nice to your dog. In this way you can be friendly and avoid having your legs scraped and your stockings laddered at the same time.

3. **Greet any other members of your household in a comparably loving fashion as well** — to avoid the dog thinking that he's the only one you're coming home to.

4. **Get all other members of your household and regular visitors to cooperate** by explaining what you are doing.

5. **Discourage any jumping up at other times** by telling your dog to keep his "Paws On The Ground!" and not proceeding with whatever it was you were planning to do (putting on his lead, throwing a toy etc.) until they are.

Tricks and Games

Tricks and games are an excellent way to keep your dog's body exercised and his mind alive. They will also provide him with an opportunity to return to 'center stage' occasionally.

The more you teach your dog, the quicker he will learn.

It doesn't matter at all whether you are teaching obedience exercises or simple tricks; with each new skill he acquires you are adding a new dimension to your lives and helping him become him a more rewarding companion to you.

A dog who knows a few tricks can also provide hours of entertainment for your child on a rainy day — and imagine how proud your child will be when your dog 'performs' in front of some friends.

It's simple, easy and rewarding, so get started and turn your dog into your very own 'Lassie'!

'Shake Hands!'

Easy to teach, this will soon become a firm favorite with everyone, as visitors immediately perceive a dog who gives his paw as harmless, cute and clever. It also procures attention for your dog which is, after all, what he loves the best.

Simply start by sitting on the floor with your dog and lightly touching a paw until he moves it. Praise and give him a treat straight away.

Repeat this many times; your dog will soon learn to lift his paw for the reward and all you have left to do is to add the instruction 'Shake Hands!' each time and to hold his paw before giving him the treat.

Jumping Over Obstacles

Every fit and healthy dog loves physical activity. Jumping over simple obstacles, through hoops or over your arms or legs is great fun for everyone and nothing could be easier to teach.

Begin by placing a simple obstacle (such as a broom handle) on the floor and encourage your dog to walk across it, giving a command such as 'Hup!' at the same time.

A piece of food thrown across the obstacle can be a good incentive for a dog to try hard at this new game.

Gradually raise the height until your dog can no longer walk comfortably across. At first he will try to clamber over the obstacle, but after a few attempts he will learn that it is easier to 'bunny hop' — this is the beginning of his show jumping career.

You can steadily increase the height and introduce different obstacles such as hula hoops, or a cardboard box for a tunnel. Great fun can be had by constructing a miniature show jumping course indoors using everyday objects such as flower pots and mop handles — one of my kids and my dogs favorite!

'Sniffer Dog'

Dogs have excellent noses and thoroughly enjoy using them. You do not have to own a Blood Hound for these games, as even the most refined pooch has a sense of smell a thousand times better than any human.

This is how to teach your dog to use his nose for a game:

Step 1. Over a period of time get your dog used to finding a favorite article ("Where's your toy? Find it!"). Start by placing the toy within easy sight and only gradually make it more difficult for your dog to find.

Step 2. Once the toy is not within sight any more, hidden behind another object or in long grass, for example, your dog will automatically start using his nose to find it.

When he sniffs for the toy and finds it reliably, you can then progress to the next stage, grandly named 'scent discrimination'.

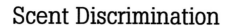

Scent Discrimination

Place the toy among some totally uninteresting, non-retrievable articles that don't smell strongly of you or your dog, such as bricks, clean, upturned dinner plates etc., and ask him to "find it". This makes it as easy as possible for your dog to pick out the right one. Only very gradually introduce other, slightly more tempting articles.

Once he can pick out his own toy reliably from a selection of other articles, you can progress to turning other objects into a 'toy' by rubbing a little of your dog's spit on them.

In this way you could mark an ace of spades in a pack of cards – totally invisible to your spectators but standing out as clear as day glow paint to your dog.

Asking all your guests to put down their car keys and telling the dog to pick out yours is another variant of this game.

Yet another 'amazing' trick is to mark a colored ball as before and have your dog pick it out among others, which will truly astound your visitors as everyone knows that dogs are color blind.

There are countless other variations to this game – the only limit is your imagination. Oh, and by the way: it can be said that my each of my children had a very unfair advantage on a leash during Easter egg hunts in the grandparent's garden!

Retrieving

Basic retrieving is one of the best and most enduring fun games for your dog, providing the thrill of the chase, physical exercise and excitement all at once. Some dogs are natural retrievers. others need a little more encouragement to begin with.

If your dog is not interested in retrieving at all, you might be able to get him to play by sitting on the floor, bouncing a ball against a wall and saying something like "Boy, this is fun! Shame Fido won't play!". Your dog might decide to join in after a time and you can build this up with lots of praise and encouragement into a proper retrieve.

Dogs who will chase the article but do not pick it up, can be motivated by trailing an old sock tied to a piece of string along the floor. Few dogs can resist trying to take a bite at this 'rat' which again can be build up into a retrieve.

Dogs who will chase and pick up the article but won't return with it can easily be taught by keeping them on the lead and exchanging the article for a piece of food, then throwing it out again straight away. Most dogs learn soon that the quicker they return the toy, the quicker they can have another go.

Apart from the fact that retrieve is perhaps the first real game your baby can begin to play with the dog, there comes a time when little babies get fascinated by dropping things and getting you to pick them up again.

Well, in my house, I got on with my writing and my old labrador saw to that for me — for hours and hours on end!

Balloons

Some dogs really love balloons and can become very adept at keeping them in the air for a long time — a great game to play indoors on a rainy day without much risk to the furniture, plus, of course, all children are endlessly fascinated with them, too.

If your dog has never encountered a balloon before, introduce him to one that is only slightly inflated and still very rubbery. This way he won't be frightened by a loud bang when he pops a balloon for the first time.

Frisbees™

A dog catching a Frisbee™ in flight is an impressive sight; furthermore, a dog who chases and retrieves Frisbees™ will never be short of exercise! Many dogs learn to do this with amazing accuracy. Teach your dog basic catching skills by throwing food or soft toys at him before you go on to something as hard as a Frisbee™.

Learning Games

Teach your dog to 'sit' as quick as lightning and to drop 'down' like a brick by playing this simple little game while watching television in your arm chair.

Hold either some food or a toy, depending which your dog prefers, and tell your dog to 'sit'. Wait patiently until he has sat, then immediately throw the food or toy to him. Your dog will learn that the quicker he responds to the word, the quicker he will get his reward. This also works for the 'down' position.

When your dog is getting good at the game, whisper the commands. A dog's hearing is much better than a humans and it will teach your dog to listen carefully to what you are saying.

If you always throw the food or toy just over his head, the dog will learn to move farther away which will give you control of the dog at a distance... this can also be turned into a game to see how far away your dog can catch something thrown by you.

APPENDIX II
Check List
"Is My Dog Safe?"

Use the Check List to pinpoint the areas where you might need to take specific action.

Go through the Check List carefully. If you are unsure about an answer, stop and test your dog's response rather than guessing what he might do.

If the answer to any question is 'No', or you're not quite sure, refer to the appropriate chapter and Action Plan for training advice.

Chapter 1

Handling

Can you touch your dog all over without him becoming aggressive or excited?

Can you bathe and brush your dog?

Can you clip his nails, hold his ears and tail without him becoming aggressive or excited?

Chapter 2

Exercise

Does your dog walk with you nicely on a loose lead?

Do you play with your dog?

Does your dog go out with other people on occasion?

Can you think of entertainments for your dog other than walks?

Chapter 3

Food.

Can you touch your dog while he's eating?

Can you take his bowl and/or bone from him without him showing any resentment?

Does he take treats without snapping?

Can you eat a meal sitting on the floor with your dog in the room?

Does your dog understand and respect a "leave it" command?

Chapter 4

Toys

Can you take a toy from your dog without him showing any resentment?

Does your dog ignore things on the floor that don't belong to him?

Can you control your dog when he is playing excitedly?

Chapter 5

Sleeping Places

Can you approach your dog in his bed without him showing any fear or resentment?

Does your dog go to his bed when you tell him to?

Does your dog have a bed in a safe place?

Can you move your dog off the furniture without him showing any resentment or fear?

Can you move your dog easily when he is sleeping on the floor?

Chapter 6

Jealousy & Attention

Can you ignore your dog for some time without him trying to gain your attention?

Can you cuddle a cushion without your dog trying to push in?

Is your dog used to being left behind when you go out?

Do you sometimes praise your dog when he is just being good and quiet?

Do you engage in any structured "special time" with your dog?

Chapter 7

Hygiene

Is your dog inoculated?

Has your dog been wormed recently?

Is your dog clean and free of fleas and mites?

Is your dog in good health and condition?

Can you get by without having to brush and comb your dog for a month?

Chapter 8

Safety

Do you have a dog guard, harness or crate in your car?

Are you always fully confident and unafraid yourself when dealing with your dog?

Have you given thought how to separate your dog and baby when you are busy?

Does your dog greet people without jumping up?

Can you run with your dog without him trying to jump at you or bite your ankles?

APPENDIX III
HOME BIRTH

On the cover of the best-selling **"Home Birth Hand Book"** there is a dog on the bed with the mother and her newborn.

For my last child, I decided to have a home birth for all kinds of reasons.

As an animal behavior specialist, a part of me was also intrigued how or if my dogs would react differently to the baby arriving thus, as opposed to going away for a few days, then turning up with a baby in my arms, as was the case with my first born.

I do not profess to have a lot of scientific data on the subject, so I will tell you of my personal experiences and you may wish to draw your own conclusions.

As far as the home birth was concerned, it was a revelation. It was absolutely wonderful compared to the previous experience. An hour after the birth, me and baby Stephen took a bath in my very own bathroom, taking all the time in the world to get accustomed to each other by candlelight (!).

Later that evening, the whole family had fish and chips on the big double bed upstairs. Everything was very much more relaxed, and the baby just kind of fitted into all our lives right from the start. The dogs showed varied degrees of interest, with the females who had had puppies themselves being the most fascinated by every scent, sound or movement, and the male dog walking off as far as he could go once the baby started crying!

Two days after the big event, one after the other, the dogs became ill. The first to show any signs was my Miniature Poodle, Rani. She had an inexplicable bout of sickness and diarrhea which was so severe that I called out an emergency vet in the middle of the night — and that is saying something because I have all kinds of remedies for all kinds of things and rarely need to go to the veterinary hospital or clinic.

The next morning, my epileptic German Shepherd began having seziures worse than he'd ever had before; my old Labrador cross had chewed herself all night and made a great big sore by the base of her tail, and one of the (perfectly well house-trained) cats had soiled in the lounge.

At the time, I just dealt with it, along the lines of, "Oh dear, it never rains, it pours."

Well, a while later, when I was not quite so love struck and baby centered, it occurred to me that the various illnesses the animals had been showing were the physical aftermath of severe stress or trauma.

The degree to which the animals were affected by having been in the house while I was giving birth, was in direct correlation to the degree of their sensitivity to me, and to the depth of their bond with me.

And, with hindsight, I feel a little amazed that I never stopped to think about how the dogs would react, hearing the sounds that I made (and, let's face it, although this was a relatively quick and easy birth, I still screamed the place down in the final stages, and the whole thing took nearly eight hours from start to finish!), scenting the strange scents, seeing, hearing, sensing strangers and family alike bustling about in excitement and trepidation, and finally, the unbelievable depth in changes of emotion from myself, my husband and my eight year old son — all without the animals having any control or part in the event, and without any possibility of action to relieve the stress.

If I have another baby, I will certainly opt for a home birth. I will also make sure that my dogs are not in the house for the actual event, and after the call to the midwife I will telephone a friend to remove and care for the dogs temporarily.

I look upon this as the equivalent of taking myself off to a safe and quiet place to have my puppy, and I think if I'd done this, my whole tribe wouldn't have come down with mystery illness in the week that followed.

APPENDIX IV
Further Information

1. For help with behavior problems write to us at Dog House Publications, 18 Marlow Avenue, Eastbourne, East Sussex BN22 8SJ. We will endeavor to find a companion animal counselor who understands your particular problems, in your area if you live in the United Kingdom.

With a good counselor, most problems can be overcome in a relatively short time, and this will be affordable to you and very worthwhile.

2. For help with behavior problems in the United States, please spend a little time sorting through the huge amount of resources available to you — particularly if you are able to use the internet to do any searching. There is a wonderful article on *Selecting a Pet Behavior Specialist* located at BehavioRx by William Campbell: www.webtrail.com/petbehavior/.

In brief: have your dog given a complete physical by a veterinarian. Ask your veterinarian if there is a humane specialist that he or she would recommend to you. Call the specialist recommended and ask questions... a good specialist with be empathetic with your problem, will listen to you and ask you many questions in return about your dog's health, the history of the problem, and what steps you have taken to correct the problem either by yourself or with other assitance.

Have the behaviorst outline any program offered and know upfront where, how often, who attends, and how much will it cost. If you are not satisfied or comfortable with any information you receive, call someone else.

Dog Training Classes

If you are entirely new to dog training, please ask at your veterinarian for the telephone numbers of classes run by kind and knowledgeable people (and membership to any kind of organization is no guarantee of proficiency, because it all depends on the individual instructor's dedication and attitude). Some of the pet centers now offer public classes as well. There also may be private instructors that can be recommended to you.

Visit the classes before you decide to join and trust your intuition on whether you would like to take your dog there.

Membership of the right dog training group can lead to making many new friends from every walk of life, and a lifetime hobby.

Further Reading

Please note that many dog books still available in shops and libraries are based on old 'army style' training methods, or "scientific" wolf pack studies, which are not really applicable to modern day companion dog ownership.

The following books by Silvia Hartmann–Kent are all up to date, easy to read and very practical, as you will know if you have found this book to be of help. You can find these either on-line at Amazon.com, Dogwise.com, JandJDog.com and other online distributors OR you can contact the US Publisher directly (see below).

Training Your Dog With Love — Highly recommended, easily read and easily duplicated so your dog can be as wonderful companion to you as you decide to teach him. $14.95

Overcoming Dog Problems — You can be your dog's best behavior counselor and make both your lives better and easier with this brilliant guide to solve just about any dog behavior problem, and with many practical tips on the most common ones. $19.95

In addition, some highly recommended books by the most compassionate modern trainers are:

Fun and Games with Dogs by Roy Hunter — A real how-to in the training department! You and your dog will never run out of things to do. Step by step instructions guide you throughout. $24.95

Fun Nosework for Dogs by Roy Hunter — Your dog has a magic nose... find out how to teach him to enjoy using it! $15.95

FUNctional Dog Training by Roy Hunter — The everyday dog at home needs all kinds of manners and Roy gives the reader great intructions for at home training. $17.95

Click Here for a Well-trained Dog by Deborah A. Jones Ph.D. — A comprehensive guide to dog training for the new millennium... well illustrated and thoughtful. $24.95

Clicker Fun by Deborah A. Jones Ph.D. — Clicker training is FUN and EASY and anyone can enjoy positive results. This psychology professor is also a professional dog trainer! $19.95

To order books directly from the publisher, either write directly to Howln Moon Press, 203 State Road Eliot, ME 03903. For more information, or to place MasterCard/Visa orders, call toll free at: 1-888-349-9438.

About The Author

Silvia Hartmann-Kent was born in Germany and moved to Great Britain in 1979.

The first edition of **"Your Dog & Your Baby"** was written when she was a Member of the British Institute of Professional Dog Trainers, an Associate Member of the Association of Pet Behavior Counselors and Senior Obedience Instructor with Berwick Obedience Association, and just after the birth of her second son, Stephen.

On the front cover you can see Stephen, then aged 8 months, with Sunny, an intact 3 year old German Shepherd male.

Silvia is England's leading lecturer on loving training and communication with companion dogs, well known for her uniquely friendly and personable style which makes learning from her so easy.

Index